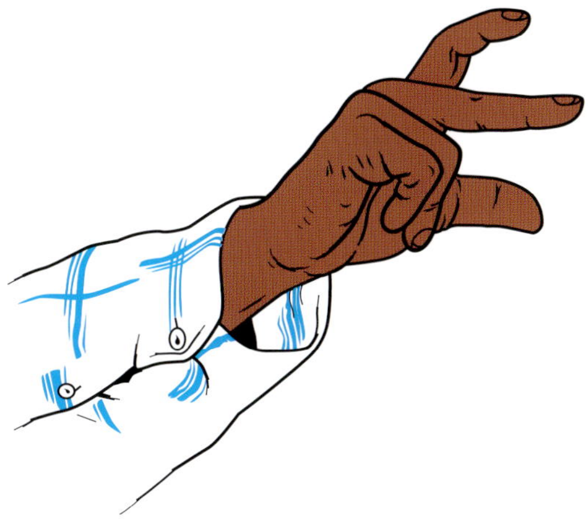

4880 Lower Valley Road • Atglen, PA 19310

Greg "Batman" Davis

ORIGINAL GANGSTER

Carver Junior High School.
1973.

RIPS
HERE
74-75

COUNT III

For a further and separate cause of action, being a different offense of the same class of crimes and offenses as the charges set forth in ALL PRECEDING COUNTS hereof, the said GREGORY DAVIS, MIKE JONES, RONALD WILLIAMS & EDWARD YOUNG

is accused by the District Attorney of and for the County of Los Angeles, State of California, by this information, of the crime of ROBBERY, in violation of Section 211, Penal Code of California, a felony, committed as follows: That the said GREGORY DAVIS, MIKE JONES, RONALD WILLIAMS & EDWARD YOUNG

on or about the 21st day of October, 1974, at and in the County of Los Angeles, State of California, did willfully, unlawfully, feloniously and by means of force and fear take personal property from the person, possession and immediate presence of

Edward Escalante.

That at the time of the commission of the above offense said defendants were armed with deadly weapons, to wit, revolvers, within the meaning of Section 12022, Penal Code.

That at the time of the commission of the offense described herein, the defendants used firearms, to wit, revolvers, within the meaning of Section 12022.5, Penal Code.

Filed in the Superior Court of the State of California, County of Los Angeles, on motion of the District Attorney of said County.

FILED

DATED: NOV 21 1974

CLARENCE E. CABELL, County Clerk

By ______ Deputy

JOSEPH P. BUSCH, District Attorney
for the County of Los Angeles, State of California

By ______ Deputy

MICHAEL A. KANNER

bnd

SUPERIOR COURT OF CALIFORNIA, COUNTY OF LOS ANGELES

January 23, 1975 Department No. 100

WILLIAM L RITZI Judge B J CRISP Clerk

L JOHNSON Reporter

APPEARANCES
(Parties and Counsel checked if present
Counsel shown opposite parties represented)

Joseph P. Busch, Jr.
District Attorney by
Deputy

Case No. A312118

X P BERMAN

THE PEOPLE OF THE STATE OF CALIFORNIA

vs

R. S. Buckley, Public Defender by
Deputy

X DAVIS, GREGORY X635186 X C SPANN

Probation is denied.

Whereas the said defendant having duly pleaded guilty of the crime of ROBBERY (Sec 211 PC), of the first degree, as charged in Count 1 of the information committed in Los Angeles County, on or about the 21st day of October 1974 and it appearing that the defendant was under the age of 21 years at the time of apprehension on the 21st day of October, 1974, to-wit: the age of 18 years, born on the 14th day of September, 1956.

IT IS THEREFORE ORDERED, ADJUDGED AND DECREED that said defendant be committed to the Youth Authority of the State of California for the term prescribed by law.

To be given credit for 96 days time served.

IT IS FURTHER ORDERED that the defendant be remanded to the custody of the Sheriff of Los Angeles County to be held in custody in the County Jail under the jurisdiction of the Youth Authority of the State of California, subject to any orders the Authority may issue.

THE MINUTE ORDER WAS
ENTERED
1-23-75
F. CABELL

[X] Remaining count(s) dismissed in the interests of justice

[ ] Bail exonerated.

COUNTY
CLERK AND CLERK OF THE
SUPERIOR COURT

PROB.
CO.J.
CYA
MISC.

YOUTH AUTHORITY COMMITMENT

"As far as the term O.G. goes, Batman is the true and living description; he is one of the original members of the first L.A. Crips gang. Batman has changed his life from being one of the most notorious figures in L.A. gang history to one of the most positive people I have ever met, trying to save the children from following his early path. He is a true inspiration, and I'm proud to call him a personal friend."

—Ice-T

Batman at Youth Authority.
1975.

ARE THE
59·62·66·68
89·97·102

Crip graffiti on the back of an apartment building.
Circa 1980.

Batman's mother, Tiny, and cousin.
1962.

Batman on Christmas morning.
Circa 1961.

Batman.
1976.

Batman.
1976.

Raymond Washington.
1976.

Crip Jackie.
1974.

Lil TQ West Side OG Crip 5.
Circa 1973.

Crazy Crip and Batman at Youth Authority.
1974.

Batman, Red Dog and Big Pepper at Youth Authority.
Circa 1975.

Baby Brother and friends.
Circa 1973.

Green Eyes.
1973.

Batman and a homegirl.
1976.

Black Ceasar, Big Swan, Batman and Crip Dog.
Circa 1975.

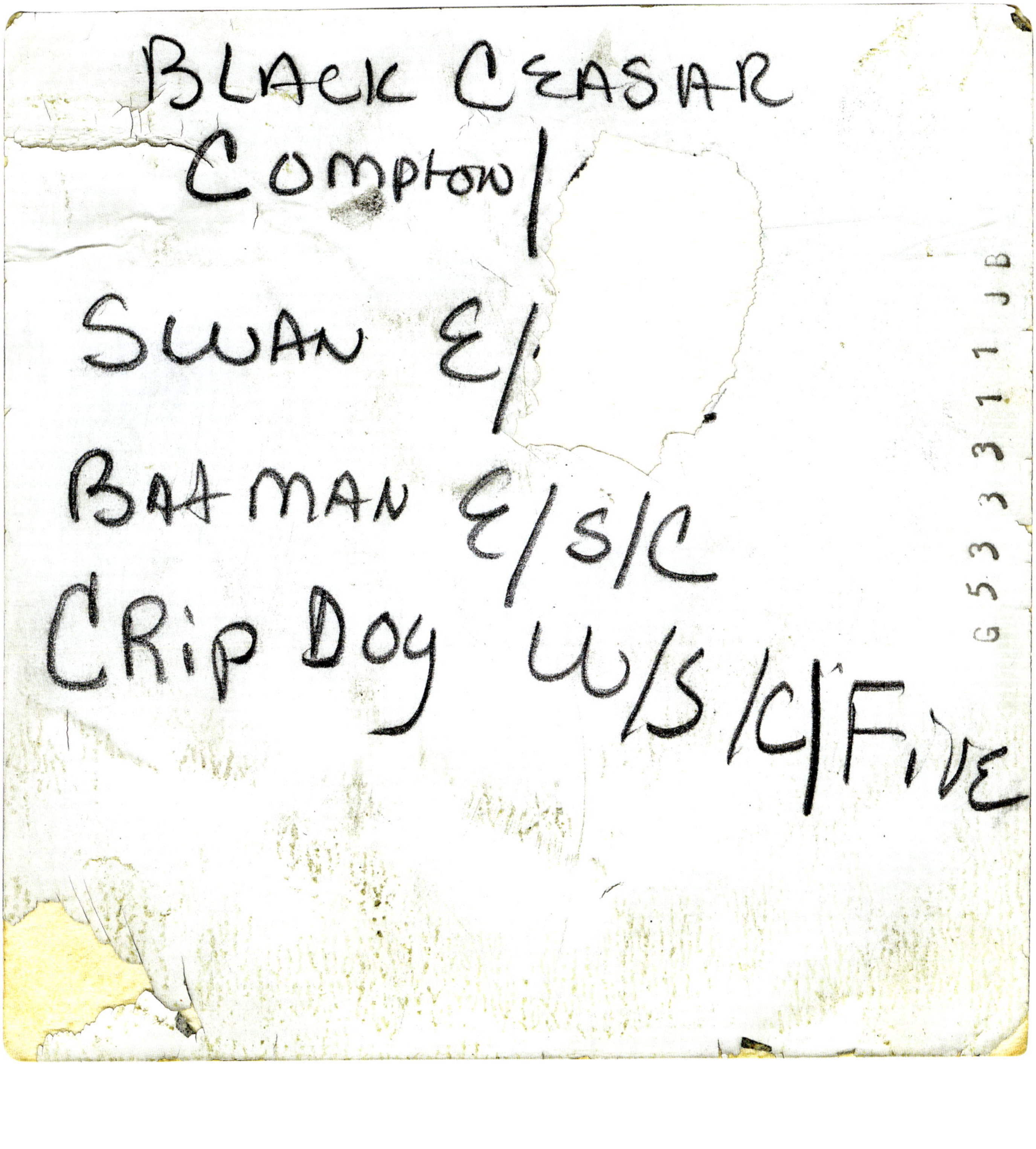
BLACK CEASAR
Compton/
SWAN E/
Batman E/S/C
CRip Dog W/S/C/Five
G53331 1JB

Mid, Crip and Blade, San Jose Crips.
1975.

Black Caesar Compton, Big Swan and Batman at Preston.
1975.

Big Pepper at Youth Authority.
Circa 1976.

Crips of Preston Youth Authority.
Circa 1976.

Al, Batman and Rochester at Youth Authority.
1975.

Batman and Sir Sweet at Youth Authority.
1976.

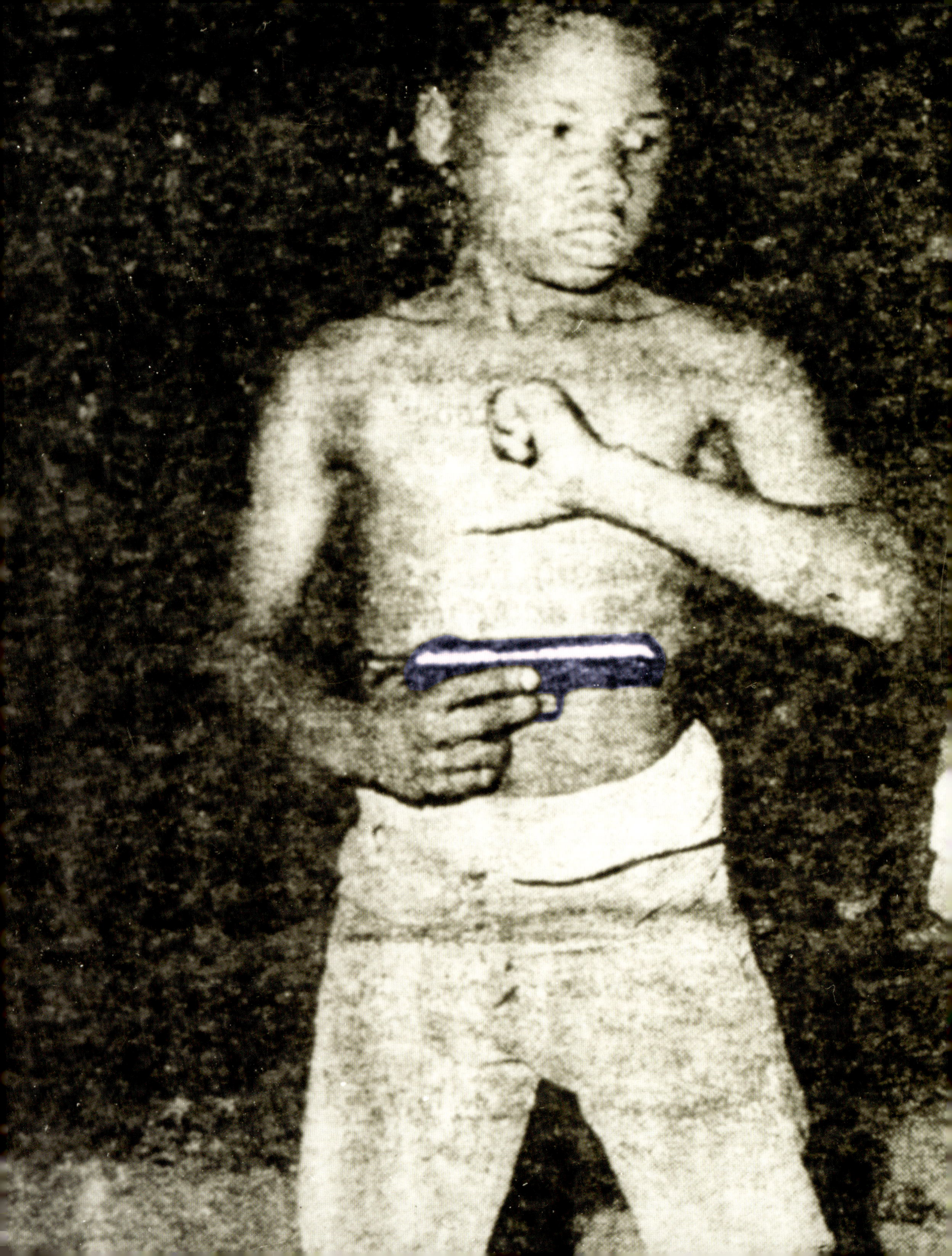

Baby Brother and friends.
1973.

Crazy Crip.
1979.

Jelly Bean, Batman and Caesar in prison.
1979.

TQ and his '64 Impala.
1976.

Big Pepper.
Circa 1975.

West Side Crips.
1976.

Buster of Castle Crips.
Circa 1973.

Batman and Baba of Black Mafia.
1978.

Cousin Phillip McCane OG W/S Crip.
Circa 1973.

Mad Hoover (second from left) and friends at the Long Tables, 45th and Broadway. 1976.

Batman in prison.
1978.

Sly of the Eastside Crips and TQ of the Harlem Crips at Youth Authority.
1974.

TQ West Side Crip 5 at Venice Beach.
1976.

Blade from San Jose Crips in Youth Authority.
Circa 1975.

Lil Crip of Venice and unknown at Youth Authority.
1975.

Gangster Love at Youth Authority.
1975.

Owl (second from left) and his homeboys in prison.
Circa 1984.

Big Pa Pa in prison.
Circa 1982.

Batman's 1963 Cadillac.
Circa 1984.

Cadillac trunk.
Circa 1981.

Batman's 1963 Chevy.
1984.

TQ in his 1964 Chevy.
1984.

Nubs, anonymous and Vamp at home on the streets.
1979.

Lil Ron and his girl.
1984.

Big C at 6-9 Apartments.
1978.

Crips.
1981.

SUPERIOR COURT OF CALIFORNIA, COUNTY OF LOS ANGELES

DEPT. NE A

Date: OCT 25, 1978

HONORABLE: ROBERT M OLSON JUDGE C KAJIKAWA Deputy Clerk

R DOUGHERTY Deputy Sheriff E AMAYA Reporter

1

A586961 (Parties and counsel checked if present)

PEOPLE OF THE STATE OF CALIFORNIA VS

01 DAVIS, GREGORY COPELAND ✓

245a 01 cts, 12021 01 cts

Counsel for People: DEPUTY DISTRICT ATTY: AARON STOVITZ ✓

Counsel for Defendant: DALE FRAILEY, DPD ✓

NATURE OF PROCEEDINGS

JURY TRIAL

Trial resumes from October 23, 1978.

At 9:30 a.m., the jury retires for further deliberation. At 10:15 a.m., the jury returns to the court, in the presence of the defendant, both counsel, alternate jurors and parties present as heretofore, with the following verdicts:

TITLE OF COURT AND CAUSE

"We, the Jury in the above-entitled action, find the Defendant GREGORY COPELAND DAVIS not guilty of ASSAULT BY MEANS OF FORCE LIKELY TO PRODUCE GREAT BODILY INJURY AND WITH DEADLY WEAPON, in violation of Section 245(a), Penal Code of California, a felony, as charged in COUNT I of the information.
This 25th day of October 1978, Donald L Milbury, Foreman

TITLE OF COURT AND CAUSE

"We the Jury in the above entitled action, find the charge against the Defendant GREGORY COPELAND DAVIS of having personally used a firearm, to wit, a handgun, within the meaning of Penal Code Section 12022.5 in the commission and attempted commission of the offense as contained in COUNT I of the Information to be not true.
This 25th day of October 1978, Donald L Milbury, Foreman

TITLE OF COURT AND CAUSE

"We, the Jury in the above-entitled action, find the Defendant GREGORY COPELAND DAVIS guilty of VIOLATION OF DANGEROUS WEAPONS' CONTROL LAW, Section 12021 Penal Code of California, a felony, as charged in COUNT II of the information.
This 25th day of October 1978, Donald L Milbury, Foreman

The verdicts are read. Pursuant to request of defendant, the jury is polled as to Count II. All twelve jurors answer in the affirmative, to the question "is this your verdict?" Verdicts are recorded. Counsel waive reading of the verdicts as recorded. The jury is discharged. Matter is referred to the Probation Department. Probation and sentence hearing is set for November 22, 1978 at 9:00 a.m. in Department NE A.

All verdict forms submitted to the jury, and instructions given and refused are filed.

REMANDED

DEPT NE A

MINUTES ENTERED 10-25-78 COUNTY CLERK

Greg 'Batman' Davis

VOLUME #1 SIXTEEN SECTIONS-SECTION A 1969 16 PAGES

Batman on Christmas morning. Circa 1961.

The Story of an Original Gangster

Gregory Davis was born in the mid-1950s in South Central Los Angeles. The eldest of five children, he lived in a one-story house with his father, an upholsterer, and stay-at-home mother. After seeing the new TV show *Batman*, 9-year-old Greg fashioned himself after the main character, tying a towel around his neck in the form of a cape. He refused to remove the cape even at school, and kept it underneath his shirt, tucked into the back of his pants. At recess, he would run into the bathroom, pull the cape out, and hang upside down from the stalls. This earned him the permanent nickname "Batman."

South Central, at the time, was a hotbed of racial tension. In the 1940s, a post-war boom in jobs caused the black population in L.A. to double. Restrictive housing covenants kept the black and white communities segregated. When blacks challenged the covenants, it angered whites, and racist groups such as the Spook Hunters attacked black residents. To protect themselves, blacks formed their own clubs.

In the 1950s and 1960s, a large number of white residents moved out of South Central. The dwindling white population led black clubs to turn against one another. With older cousins in the Businessmen and Slausons, Batman started hanging around both clubs, trying to emulate their tough behavior. When the Watts Riots erupted on August 11, 1965, Batman followed looters into a store, and loaded up his little, red wagon with candy and bottles of Silver Satin wine.

After the riots, rivalry between clubs was replaced by social awareness and political activity. One of the members of the Slausons, Bunchy Carter, founded the Los Angeles chapter of the political organization the Black Panthers. Too young to join, Batman sold copies of *The Black Panther* newspaper with pride. However, FBI Director J. Edgar Hoover targeted groups deemed subversive with his Counter Intelligence Program (COINTELPRO), destroying the Panther's leadership. Batman says, "They should have let the Black Panthers go on because there probably wouldn't be no Crips."

In the summer of 1969, 15-year-old Raymond Lee Washington founded the Baby Avenue Cribs. Raymond modeled the Cribs after the Avenues gang and the Black Panthers, incorporating leather coats into their dress code. A friend from the neighborhood, Batman was one of the original 10 members.

Shortly after joining the Cribs, Batman found a gun in a neighbor's tool cabinet and was caught shooting at the dogs. Despite the punishment he received from his father, this incident sparked Batman's lifelong fascination with guns. Using a BB gun, pipe and some rubber bands, he made his first zip gun, a .38 pistol. But, when his friend tested it, the gun malfunctioned, and split his ear in half. Batman went back to the drawing board, and made a longer-barreled .410 design. This time it worked. He continued to make the .410 model and, after getting caught by the sheriff's department twice, was given the nickname "Crazy .410." "I liked it when they used to holler, 'Crazy .410, come here!'" Batman says in his deep, smoky voice. "I thought it was kind of cool."

> "They should have let the Black Panthers go on because there probably wouldn't be no Crips."

By 1971, the Cribs no longer resembled a political group, and were a full-fledged gang involved in fights and robberies. Looking to expand, Raymond approached Stanley "Tookie" Williams to found the Westside set of the Cribs, and also added a Compton set. Besides the leather jackets, which were often obtained through robberies, their dress code included ace deuce hats, earrings in their left ears, suspenders, gloves on their left hands and canes. In 1972, a newspaper article described several members involved in an assault as young cripples. The description caught on, and the Cribs became the Crips.

After he was expelled from numerous schools for fighting, 16-year-old Batman was sent to Job Corps in Salt Lake City, Utah. Although he previously had no interest in sports—"I didn't want to play that stuff. Shit, I was a gangster"—while in Job Corps, he took up boxing and karate. He also took up breaking into the soda machines. After getting caught by a counselor, he was given two options: to go to the on-site jail or take a bus back to L.A. Batman chose to go back home, where he started "Crippin' to the fullest."

Batman had only been away at Job Corps for a few months, but when he got back to Los Angeles, things had already changed. During the summer of 1972 *Super Fly* had come out, and everyone was wearing wide-brimmed hats like the movie's main character, Youngblood Priest. On the streets, more sets had branched off the original Eastside, Westside and Compton Crips, and one of the Compton sets, the Pirus, weren't Crips anymore.

The Pirus had never liked being under Mac Thomas, the leader of the Compton Crips, but had put up with it until Tookie fought one of them at Centennial High School. "I don't know exactly who it was, but Tookie hit a top dog from the set, and knocked him through the window," Batman explains. "And after that, they said they weren't gonna be Crips anymore, they was gonna be Piru, from the name of their street. Quite naturally: Ya'll supposed to be homies and somebody come up and do something like that—what do you expect? So they started their own thing, the Pirus."

"Ya'll supposed to be homies and somebody come up and do something like that—what do you expect?"

The Pirus turned against the Crips, and became their own gang, getting others such as the Brims, Bounty Hunters and Outlaws to join them. This was the beginning of the Bloods, the Crips' archenemy, and it didn't take long for the violence between gangs to start.

One afternoon, Batman and his friend Jackrabbit were hanging out at the hamburger stand across the street from Fremont High School. Fremont was one of the many schools Batman had been kicked out of before getting sent to Job Corps, and where Raymond, his best friend and the leader of the whole Crip nation, still went. Jackrabbit and Batman were sitting on top of one of the cement tables, drinking sodas, when a police car pulled up.

One of the officers asked why they weren't in school, but neither Batman nor Jackrabbit came up with a good answer. The officers handcuffed them, put them in the backseat of the squad car, and drove around for a while. "So they rolled down to 80th street, and got us out the backseat, un-handcuffed us, and said over the loudspeaker, 'We got some Crips,' and then took off. I kept tellin' Jackrabbit, 'I ain't worried about it, ain't nobody out.' But it was somebody out."

Batman at Youth Authority. 1975.

Batman and Jackrabbit almost made it to the corner, when several Swans appeared out of nowhere. Batman recalls, "One of them said, 'Ain't your name Batman?' and I said, 'Nah.' 'Ain't you a Crip?' 'Nah.' 'I'ma ask you one more time: Is your name Batman?' I said, 'Yeah.' 'Ain't you a Crip?' 'Yeah.' And when I said that, I knew what I had to do. I punched the one that was talking to me, and the next thing I know, someone on the sideline hit me on the side of my face with a shotgun. 'Don't fuck with a Main Street Swan, Blood,' that's what he told me. 'We ought to kill your ass.'"

But with that warning, the Swans turned and walked away, leaving Batman bloody on the pavement. Jackrabbit had taken off running when Batman threw the first punch, so Batman started making his way out of Swan territory on his own.

Batman headed toward the high school, and when he got there, he saw Crip Jackie and her sister Pam. Jackie was the head of the Criplettes, the Crips' all-girl set. The Criplettes also had a dress code—khaki pants, turban hats and bleached-blond hair—and were just as bad as their male counterparts. They would steal peoples' leather coats and fight girls from other gangs like the Brimlettes, Piru Girls and Lady Laws.

"They said, 'What happened to you?' 'Man, them motherfuckers caught me; they beat me up.' So they called the ambulance for me, 'cause the whole inside of my mouth was busted open, and the paramedic told me I needed to go to the hospital, but I said, 'No, I ain't going to no hospital.' So I went home. When I got home, I was hidin' it so my mother couldn't see it, but the next day, when I was lookin' in the mirror, she was like, 'What happened? Somebody done whooped your ass, huh? Bout time you got your ass whooped. Keep your ass at that school.' But I said to myself, 'Yeah, but I'm gonna get them, though. They ain't gonna get away with that.' And they didn't get away either. I waited a whole week, but I got them back. That's all that matters, I got 'em back."

"And they didn't get away either. I waited a whole week, but I got them back. That's all that matters, I got 'em back."

In 1973, Raymond was sentenced to three years in prison for robbery. Without his leadership, the violence on the streets went from bad to worse.

One afternoon, Batman was hanging out with his sister, two of her girlfriends and Charles Ray at the park. Charles Ray was his sister's boyfriend at the time. He was also a member of the Avalon Crips, and he wore his hair in a big, natural afro. Batman's homeboy Tick drove by, and they all piled into his red 1966 Chevy lowrider with the white chrome tips. Tick was brown skinned with buckteeth. They cruised around and for a while, listening to music.

"We go by the 60 Laws neighborhoods, and I could see they were giving a party at one of the houses," Batman explains. "So I hollered out the window, 'Nigga this Crip! Fuck a Outlaw!' They say, 'Fuck a Crip!' 'Fuck your momma, motherfucker! Crip or die!' I'm just straight hoo-bangin'—Crip this, Crip that. Next thing I know, I see a big ol' light come from behind the bush, and a shotgun blast hits the car. Then all kinds of guns start goin' off. Charles Ray steps on it, but he got his head down, and all of a sudden—bang!—he hits a tree. The electric doors wasn't workin', so we bailed out the windows, haulin' ass. Nobody got hurt, but I ain't never do that shit no more."

Tick got his car fixed, and a week later, he and Batman went to visit a girl Batman was seeing at the time. She lived in the Devil's Lane neighborhood—dangerous territory for Crips to be in. They parked outside her Spanish bungalow-style house and while they were waiting for her to come out, two gangsters approached the car. Batman explains, "One of them said, 'What's up, Blood?' I said, 'Hey, what's up?' They said, 'This ain't nothin' but a Lane and Park thang, fuck a nigga with an earring.' They was talking 'bout us Crips. Dangle earrings with crosses on the end were part of our dress code. I was like, 'Well, I'm not down with that.' I didn't want to get into it in front of the girl's house. They kept hoo-bangin' for a minute, but then they walked on. When the girl came out, I told her we had to go. Tick drove in their direction, and I hopped in the backseat and rolled down the window. When we caught up to them, I said, 'Chitty chitty bang bang, fuck a Lane and Park thang! This Crip, motherfucker!' I pulled out my nickel-plated .38 revolver and started shooting at them, and they went runnin'."

Batman and Tick kept on driving, until they came across a line of candy-colored lowriders on Broadway. "Tick said, 'We gonna follow them.' I said, 'Nah, don't follow them, we ain't going with them.' 'Yeah, man, they goin' to a party.' Tick was trying to catch him a woman. I say, 'Don't follow them.' He started following these dudes anyways, and when they hit the corner, I could tell they were Bloods. I told Tick, 'These the Park Boys!' Tick say, 'These the homeboys.' 'Man, these motherfuckers are not the homeboys. These motherfuckers are Bloods!' They start parking there cars, and I said, 'Tick, don't park this motherfuckin' car. Keep goin'.' As soon as he tried to keep goin', they like, 'Blood, where you goin', Blood? There's a spot right there.' And I said, 'Didn't I tell you them wasn't the homeboys? Nigga, punch this car!' So he started driving real fast, and they started chasing us. I jumped in the backseat; rolled down the window. They started shooting at us, and I'm shooting back—it's just back and forth, back and forth. We hittin' dips and everything—whoop! We was very lucky, them Parks was unloading on our ass, and one of the bullets hit the gas tank and knocked a hole in it, and we didn't know it. When we got to my house, Tick started his car, and he was like, 'Man, ain't no gas in this motherfucker.' So we looked up under there with a flashlight, and he had a hole in the gas tank!" Batman laughs. "He got mad at me about that! 'Man you ain't gonna ride in my car, man. Every time my car gets shot up!'"

That summer, all the Crips were planning to go the Watts Festival. Created in 1966, one year to the month after the Watts Riots, the festival is an annual two-day event that still goes on today. Over the years, it has featured performers such as James Brown, Stevie Wonder, WAR, Richard Pryor and Barry White. "I can't remember who was playing that summer, but I didn't give a damn back then," Batman says. "I wasn't going there for the music."

Before the festival, Rosey Grier called a meeting with all the Crips to talk about being peaceful at the event. Rosey was a retired pro-football player and a respected community activist, so Crips from allover Los Angeles attended the meeting at Charles Drew Middle School.

Rosey started the meeting by saying that the festival was a special event meant to uplift the community, and then asked the Crips not to cause any problems at the festival. "We all agreed," Batman says, "but being that we were so young, it went in one ear and out the other."

"The festival was at a big park at 103rd and Century," Batman continues. "I was at the festival, and the Bounty Hunters were trying to lead me into that alley. 'C'mon back here, Blood, if you wanna get down.' So I was like, fuck it, I'm gonna go back there. Everybody kept saying, don't go back there, they gonna shoot you, don't go back there. So they finally came on out and came in the park. So right in the park we get into it with them. We start fightin' and all that shit. So me, Earthquake and a couple others get handcuffed and they take us to jail."

The police took them to jail all the way in Huntington Park, and threw them in a cell where they stayed overnight. The next morning, they went to court and were charged with trespassing and disturbing the peace. The public defender told them if they pled guilty, they would be credited for time served and released. So they all pled guilty, and were let go.

The Watts Festival was still going on, and Batman wanted to go back to it. "I went home first and changed my clothes. I put on my beige khaki suit, added white suspenders, which I wore dropped, and a white ace deuce hat. Then I tucked a .410 zip gun into my pants. I met up with my boy Stanley from the Avalon Crips. Stanley was dark skinned, bowlegged and could talk a gang of shit. We were going to go get Charles Ray at his house, so we took the bus to 46th and Central, and decided to walk the rest of the way since I knew a shortcut. But before we got there, I happened to turn around and see a police car coming toward us.

"I took the zip gun out of my pants, and threw it under a nearby car so that they wouldn't find it if they searched us. The police stopped us, and started asking us questions. They didn't see me throw the zip gun, but there was a man across the street who had been watering his lawn, and he told them to look under the car. One of the officers got on his hands and knees and looked under the car, grabbed the zip gun and threw it on the hood of the police car. 'Who does this pipe belong to?' He thought the zip gun was just a pipe, but that wasn't much better since a pipe is still considered a deadly weapon. 'It ain't mine,' I said. 'It ain't mine either,' Stanley said. They handcuffed both of us, and put us in the back of the police car. They took us to the Newton police station, and handcuffed us to a bench. We sat there for a while, and then they took us into the interrogation room. By then, they had figured out that the pipe was actually a zip gun, and we were asked again whom it belonged to. Again, we both denied that it was ours. 'Empty your pockets,' the detective demanded. I had a Hot Tamale box in my pocket, and when I dropped it on the table it made a loud thud. 'What do we have here?' He grabbed the box and opened it, dumping its contents out. One by one, the .410 shells hit the table. 'So,' he said, 'that's your gun.' I spent a little time in juvenile hall for that offense, and while I was in there, I thought about all I had been going through, and knew I needed to change."

Batman decided to start going to church with them his friend, Kenny, who came from a spiritual family. The church was the People's Temple, and Batman listened carefully as Jim Jones spoke about the Promised Land. He said that the Promised Land was a place where there would be no worries or problems, and Batman imagined a place where he wouldn't get in any more in trouble or have to go back to juvenile hall.

"After the service, Kenny asked me, 'Man, you wanna go the Promised Land?' I said, 'Can we take the car?' 'Nah, we can't take the car.' 'I don't really wanna go if we can't take the car.' 'Was you listening? Jim Jones said we don't need nothin'. When we go the Promised Land, all of our worries will be over.' I said, 'This sounds cool.'"

But that night, Batman headed to a concert. Just as he got there, his homies Mike, Mr. T and Speedy pulled up in nice cars: a pretty, white 1950 Chevy, a Lincoln Continental with the suicide doors, and a 1963 Impala. "I said, 'How'd ya'll get these cars?' Mike said, 'Fool, we been out robbin'.' I said, 'Shit, I need me a car. I'm goin' with you next time.' 'Alright, you can go with us next Sunday.'"

Mad Hoover (second from left) and friends at the Long Tables, 45th and Broadway. 1976.

The following Sunday, Batman met up with them at Mike's house. They waited for it to get dark, and then went out on a robbing spree. The first man Batman tried to rob laughed at him. "I wanted to blast him," Batman says, "but the gun jammed." Then they found a dark place to hide in, and when people walked by they took everything they could. When they ran out of room in Mike's truck, they decided to head back.

"The police came from nowhere," Batman says. "They pulled us over, and said, 'Get out, back up, lay down,' and they made us lay down in the dirt. I had on a brand new khaki suit, so I was in the pushup position. One of the police came and put his foot on my back, making me lay down in the dirt. They arrested us, and that was my first time going to Youth Authority. The Promised Land was over."

The gun had been stashed under Batman's seat, so he ended up getting the most time. He was sentenced to 18 months and sent to Preston School of Industry, a California Youth Authority correctional facility for offenders age 14 to 25, in Ione, California. Preston was rougher than any facility he had been in before. There were constant fights, especially between whites and blacks.

There were too many fights to recount, but there were two that stood out to Batman. One occurred after a white boy said some things to a Hoover Crip named Pepper that he shouldn't have. That fight turned into a racial riot, and prolonged a lot of peoples' stays in Preston, including Batman's. The other fight occurred when Batman ran into the Main Street Swan who had hit him on the side of my face with the butt of the shotgun. "I asked him, 'Do you remember me?' He said, 'Nah.' I said, 'I'm Batman.' We started fighting right there in the mess hall. I got sent to the hole for that fight, but it was worth it."

In the summer of 1976, Batman was released. "If I knew what I know now, I would have never got myself caught up like that," he says. "I would have did like some of them other guys did and left it alone before they got too deep. Some left it alone after they went to YA. Me? I carried on."

To help Batman stay out of trouble, his parole officer got him a job at the Watts Labor Community Action Committee (WLCAC), a nonprofit organization that serves the people of South Central Los Angeles. The WLCAC was in Blood territory, and sometimes the Bounty Hunters would come around on payday and take people's earnings. Batman wasn't going to let them take his money, so he started to carry a nickel-plated .38 in a brown paper bag with his lunch.

Robert H. Philibosian, Chief Assistant Attorney General, S. Clark Moore, Assistant Attorney General, Edward T. Fogel, Jr., and Vincent J. O'Neill, Deputy Attorneys General, for Plaintiff and Respondent.

Defendant was charged with: (count I) assault with a deadly weapon, in violation of subdivision (a) of section 245 of the Penal Code; and (count II) possession by an ex-convict of a concealable weapon, in violation of section 12021 of the Penal Code. After a trial by jury, he was acquitted on count I but found guilty on count II. He was sentenced to state prison for the middle term of two years. He has appealed; we affirm.

During a high school picnic, the victim was shot by someone, alleged to have been the defendant. The defense was an alibi. In support of that alibi[1/], the defense produced several persons

---

1/

The affirmative evidence in support of the alibi was from defendant himself, his brother and his father. The importance of independent corroboration is obvious.

"So one night, I saw the police coming toward me, and I took the gun and threw it," Batman says. "I guess he caught the glare of the gun in his headlights. He pulled up, and he said, 'Hey Batman!' I say, 'What's up, man?' He was like, 'What was that you threw?' I said, 'Oh, I ain't throw nothin'.' He say, 'Yeah, I seen you throw something. If I got to get out the car and go get it, I'm taking your ass to jail.' Now mind you, I just got out of Y.A. I said, 'Alright, man.' He say, 'And when you pick it up, pick it up from the butt of the gun.' So I went and picked it up, and he said, 'Now put it in your pocket.' I put it in my pocket, and he said, 'You know they got a hit on you, you gonna need that gun,' and he took off."

> "Now put it in your pocket. You know they got a hit on you, you gonna need that gun."

A couple of months after Batman started working at the WLCAC, he got a call from Raymond. Raymond had just been released from prison. Raymond was Batman's best friend, and he hadn't told anybody else he was out yet. Batman and Raymond met up and decided to go to Centinela Park—a park in Inglewood where everybody used to hang out at—and surprise everyone.

On the walk there, Raymond didn't have too much to say about prison—he had always been on the quiet side—but did say he never wanted to go back. He said that nobody liked the Crips in prison, and that they were outnumbered. Then Batman filled Raymond in about what had been going on, and told him that some people had been claiming that they were the leader of the Crips.

When they got to Centinela Park, everyone just stared. Raymond had always been muscular, but now he was huge. He was also three years older, but looked like he had aged much more than that. "It was a shock to the whole Crip nation," Batman says. "Nobody knew what to say. They just kept looking at him and looking at me, and they were hoping I didn't fill him in about what was going on."

Raymond could have fought all of them: "He could slang them thangs," Batman says. But Raymond didn't have fight to take back his place; he didn't have to say anything either. His presence was enough to put people back in line. "When they say you's the leader of your set, that's for your neighborhood," Batman says, "but when it came to the big meetings and stuff like that, the Crips only had one boss, and that was Raymond. He was the leader of the whole cha cha."

The next weekend, Raymond wanted to go visit some of the homeboys who lived in Gardena. Neither Raymond nor Batman had cars at the time, so Batman asked Raymond how they were going to get there, and Raymond said they were going to walk. "'Walk? From 76th Street to Gardena? Do you know how many blocks we have to walk through to get there? We have to cross Central, San Pedro, Vermont, Main, Broadway, Western...' That meant crossing through different gangs' territory. 'That's right,' Raymond said. So I said, 'Well, OK. I got to go to the house before we walk anywhere.' So when I get to the house, Raymond waited outside, and I went in the house and got a sawed-off shotgun. I put it in my pants, and said, 'Let's go.' So we're walking, and when we get to San Pedro, I said, 'Raymond, check this out, man. I got this shotgun.' 'Man, what you doing with that? We don't need no gun!' That's when he took my gun, and he threw it in the storm drain. 'Why'd you do that shit, man?' 'Man, we can fight!' I said, 'Fool, don't nobody fight no more!' Raymond had been in prison for three years, and when he got out, everything had changed. The game that Raymond put together was over."

Raymond didn't understand how much the streets had changed while he was in prison. When he got locked up, people were still settling problems with their fists, but now everybody had a gun. Raymond wanted to call a truce, but it was too late. He had created the Crips, but the snowballing violence would prove to be out of his control.

In 1978, Batman was charged with assault with a deadly weapon, a crime he did not commit. The jury returned with a not guilty verdict on the assault charge, but because he was an ex-convict in possession of a concealable weapon when he was arrested, Batman, now 18, was sentenced to two years in state prison.

On August 9, 1979, while Batman was serving his sentence, Raymond Washington was shot and killed at the intersection of 64th and San Pedro streets in L.A. "I would have been right there with him, but I was locked up," Batman says. "God works in his own ways." Raymond's murder marked the end of an era, and the start of more violence and drugs.

After being released from prison in 1980, Batman ran into one of his homeboys on the street. While he was talking to him, Batman watched as cars pulled up to his homeboy, who dipped a stick into a bottle of clear liquid, gave it to the person in the car, and was handed cash in return. Batman asked what he was selling, and his homeboy told him "water." "I'm like, 'I'll be right back,'" Batman recalls. "So I went and found a bottle, and turned the water on. He asked, 'What are you doing?' I said, 'I'm going to sell me some water too.' And he started laughing, 'Nah, it ain't that kind of water, man. This is PCP.'" And with that, Batman entered the drug trade.

Batman and RP. 1985.

Batman sold PCP until he was charged with murder in 1983. When the police attempted to execute the warrant at his parent's house, Batman was not there. The police seized items belonging to Batman, including handguns, shotguns, rifles, shells, cartridges, magazines, stereo equipment, a radio scanner, triple-beam scale, three photo albums and a blue bandana. Facing life in prison, Batman prayed to God. "I got down on my knees in front of all these Crips, and asked God to help me. I said, 'I know I got to go back to prison, but please don't let me do all that time.' And the homeboys looked at me and said, 'Cuz, why you down there praying to that white God? Nigga, you goin' to the pen.' I said, 'I'm going, but I ain't gonna be there as long as you.'" Batman's prayers were answered, and he was found not guilty on the murder charge, and given just two years for the weapons.

Upon entering prison, Batman met an old friend, Bobby Joe Maxwell. While he was talking to Bobby, a group of Bloods started threatening Batman, who was still shackled at the hands and feet. Bobby stood up and told the Bloods, "This is my homeboy, we from the same neighborhood," and the Bloods backed down. Batman asked, "Why are they scared of you? You ain't a gangster!" Bobby replied, "Boy, I'm the Skid Row Stabber"—a serial killer who targeted homeless people in Los Angeles. It was also during this prison stint that Batman befriended serial killer Charles Manson. "They say he's racist, but he didn't seem racist," Batman says. "I used to sit on the bench down low and he'd sit up high and we used to just talk."

Pressed for cash after his release in 1985, Batman took an Uzi and planned to rob some high rollers. But he was stopped by one of them whose life he had unknowingly saved in a gang shootout. To thank him, the high roller gave Batman $2,500, a brand new .357 magnum and a half kilo of cocaine. Off to a good start, Batman re-entered the drug game.

A year later, Batman met Fast Eddie, the owner of a local restaurant known as The Steakhouse, who encouraged Batman to change his life around. Shortly after, Batman stopped selling drugs and started hanging out at Fast Eddie's restaurant. It was at The Steakhouse that Karen, his future wife, finally gave him her number. They had met a few times before, once at a gas station when Karen was having a bad day. "I was telling him, 'You're Crippin' and you're 30 years old, you don't need to be doing this.' He was wearing a big coat, and I pushed him, and his chest was so big, his arms were gigantic, he was huge! I touched his chest, and I was like, Oh Jesus, I'm gonna die right now. I just hit this man they call Batman. They already say he's a killer, a kidnapper, a murderer and a dope dealer. He's gonna kill me."

"I was telling him, 'You're Crippin' and you're 30 years old, you don't need to be doing this.'"

Batman. 1985.

The Steakhouse often had live performances by blues acts, which drew an older crowd. Through spending time there, Batman realized he needed to grow up. He met with a bishop, and started attending church. "I started seeing things change from me being violent to something positive," he says. In 1991, a neighbor gave Batman ex-football player and actor Jim Brown's number. Batman met with Brown, and subsequently started working with his Amer-I-Can Program. Batman felt he had found his calling, and dedicated himself to helping others.

Batman and Karen were married in 1994. The wedding, which took place at Jim Brown's house in the Hollywood Hills, was attended by rapper Ice-T, and received coverage in *The New York Times* and international newspapers. Throughout the late 1990s, Batman continued to work with Amer-I-Can, as well as with Project Corner Stone, Family Helpline and Jeopardy, the LAPD's gang intervention program, and spoke in schools and prisons around the country. In 2000, Batman established Let's Save the Babies, a non-profit organization that provides counseling to at-risk youth, promotes education and implements community programs. He has received countless awards and trophies for his work.

Forty years after the Crips were founded, Batman, now 52, resides in a Southern California suburb. Except for tattoos of three teardrops under his left eye and "Original Crip" on his neck, Batman hardly resembles the bandana wearing, gun-slinging man he once was. His story almost sounds like an urban legend—but he has the photos and police record to prove it.

66 FORM CR 29

SUPERIOR COURT OF CALIFORNIA, COUNTY OF LOS ANGELES

COURT ID. 1 9 0 0 0 5

BRANCH NORTHEAST DIV.

FOR COURT USE ONLY

PEOPLE OF THE STATE OF CALIFORNIA versus

DEFENDANT: 01 DAVIS GREGORY COPELAND [X] Present [ ] Not Present

AKA:

COMMITMENT TO STATE PRISON P.C. § 1170

ABSTRACT OF JUDGMENT

CASE NUMBER: A 586961

Hearing 11-22-78 Dept. No. NEA Judge ROBERT M OLSON Clerk C KAJIKAWA

Reporter E AMAYA Counsel for People A STOVITZ

Counsel for Defendant D. FRAILEY Probation Number or Probation Officer UNK

1. Defendant was convicted of the commission of the following crimes:

[ ] Additional counts are listed on attachment 1.a.

Count	Code	Section No.	Crime	Date of Conviction Mo. Day Yr.	Conviction by: Jury Trial	Court Trial	Plea	Count Stayed PC § 654	ENHANCEMENTS Charged and Found: PC § 12022 (a) or (b)	PC § 12022.5	PC § 12022.6 (a) or (b)	PC § 12022.7	Additional term stricken due circumstances in mitigation: PC § 12022	PC § 12022.5	PC § 12022.6	PC § 120
02	PC	12021	ASSAULT BY MEANS OF FORCE	10-25-78	x											

2. A. Number of prior prison terms charged and found: 0 667.5(c) felonies; 0 other than 667.5(c) felonies.

B. Punishment for prior prison terms stricken: ____ 667.5(c) felonies; ____ other than 667.5(c) felonies.

3. The crime with the greatest "principal" term of imprisonment (including § 12022-series enhancements) is:

A. [ ] In the present proceeding, Count 02. B. [ ] In a prior uncompleted sentence identified on next line.

COUNTY ____ CASE NUMBER ____ COUNT CODE ____ SECTION NUMBER ____ CRIME AND DEGREE ____ DATE OF CONVICTION MO. DAY YEAR

4. Defendant is sentenced on the crime with the greatest "principal" term to state prison for the [ ] lower [X] middle [ ] upper base term of 2 / years

5. Unstayed and unstricken enhancements imposed:

A. [ ] Penal Code § 12022(a) [ ] Penal Code § 12022(b) [ ] Penal Code § 12022.5 [ ] Penal Code § 12022.7 .... ____ years

B. [ ] Penal Code § 12022.6(a) [ ] Penal Code § 12022.6(b) .... ____ years

C. [ ] Penal Code § 667.5(a) .... ____ years

D. [ ] Penal Code § 667.5(b) .... ____ years

E. Terms for consecutive sentences: ____ years

(1) [ ] Other convictions in the present case for felonies not listed in § 667.5(c) on counts ____ .... 0 / years

(2) [ ] Other convictions in prior uncompleted sentences for felonies not listed in § 667.5(c)

COUNTY ____ CASE NUMBER ____ COUNTS ____ .... 0 / years

(3) [ ] Other convictions in the present case for felonies listed in § 667.5(c) on counts ____ .... 0 / years

(4) [ ] Other convictions in prior uncompleted sentences for felonies listed in § 667.5(c)

COUNTY ____ CASE NUMBER ____ COUNTS ____ .... 0 / years

Concurrent Sentences (to be served with sentence on count identified on line 3):

A. [ ] For convictions of the present case, counts ____. B. [ ] For convictions of prior uncompleted sentence.

Of years imposed above on lines 4 through 5.E.(4), number of years stayed pursuant to California Rules of Court, Rule 447, to comply with Penal Code §§ 1170.1(a) [5-year limit] and 1170.1(f) [double-base-term limit] .... (0 / years

The total unstayed prison term imposed by this judgment is .... 2 / years

Execution of sentence imposed: A. [X] at initial sentencing hearing B. [ ] at resentencing pursuant to decision on appeal

C. [ ] after revocation of probation D. [ ] at resentencing pursuant to recall of commitment (P.C. § 1170(d))

The court pronounced sentence on 1 1 2 2 7 8 (MO. DAY YEAR). Defendant is credited for time spent in custody, 231 total days, including:

Actual Local Time 231 P.C. § 4019(b) credit ____, State Institutions Time ____ (specify dates of admission and release in oral proceedings and minutes).

Defendant is remanded to the custody of the Sheriff to be delivered: [X] forthwith [ ] after 48 hours, excluding Saturdays, Sundays and Holidays

into the custody of the Director of Corrections at the Reception-Guidance Center located at [ ] Calif. Institution for Women – Frontera

[ ] Calif. Medical Facility – Vacaville [X] Calif. Institution for Men – Chino [ ] Other: (specify) ____

ORDER DATE JAN 1_ 1979 ... PERMIT ...

CLERK OF SUPERIOR COURT

I hereby certify the foregoing to be a correct abstract of the judgment made in this action.

By M. Miller DEPUTY

Date 11-22-78

This form is prescribed pursuant to Penal Code § 1213.5 to satisfy the requirements of Penal Code § 1213 (Abstract of Judgment and Commitment) for determinate sentences under Penal Code § 1170. A copy of probation report shall accompany the Department of Corrections' copy of this form pursuant to Penal Code § 1203c. A copy of the sentencing proceedings and any supplementary probation report shall be transmitted to the Department of Corrections pursuant to Penal Code 1203.01. Attachments may be used but must be incorporated by reference.

Form Adopted by the Judicial Council of California Revised Effective October 1, 1978

ABSTRACT OF JUDGMENT-COMMITMENT

FORM CR 290

Pen C. 667.5, 1170, 1170.1, 1213.5, 12022, 12022.5, 12022.6, 12022.7.

SUPERIOR COURT OF CALIFORNIA, COUNTY OF LOS ANGELES

People of the State of California PLAINTIFF(S)

vs.

ORY COPELAND DAVIS DEFENDANT(S)

CASE NUMBER A586961 DEPARTMENT NUMBER NE A

VERDICT (Guilty)

he Jury in the above-entitled action, find the Defendant GREGORY COPELAND DAVIS of ASSAULT BY MEANS OF FORCE LIKELY TO PRODUCE GREAT BODILY INJURY WITH DEADLY WEAPON, in violation of Section 245(a), Penal Code of fornia, a felony,

ged in COUNT I of the information

FILED
OCT 25 1978
JOHN J. CORCORAN, Acting County Clerk
BY C. KAJIKAWA, DEPUTY

day of 19__,

Foreman

210 8-75 VERDICT (Guilty)

SUPERIOR COURT OF CALIFORNIA, COUNTY OF LOS ANGELES

The People of the State of California PLAINTIFF(S)

vs.

GREGORY COPELAND DAVIS DEFENDANT(S)

CASE NUMBER A586961 DEPARTMENT NUMBER NE A

VERDICT (Not Guilty)

We, the Jury in the above-entitled action, find the Defendant GREGORY COPELAND DAVIS not guilty of VIOLATION OF DANGEROUS WEAPONS' CONTROL LAW, Section 12021, Penal Code of California, a felony, as charged in COUNT II of the information.

FILED
OCT 25 1978
JOHN J. CORCORAN, Acting County Clerk
BY C. KAJIKAWA, DEPUTY

This ____ day of ____ 19__,

Foreman

VERDICT (Not Guilty)

76V225 12-77
C128

SUPERIOR COURT OF CALIFORNIA, COUNTY OF LOS ANGELES

People of the State of California PLAINTIFF(S)

vs.

EGORY COPELAND DAVIS DEFENDANT(S)

CASE NUMBER A586961 DEPARTMENT NUMBER NE A

VERDICT (Guilty)

the Jury in the above-entitled action, find the Defendant GREGORY COPELAND DAVIS y of ASSAULT, in violation of Section 240, Penal Code of California, felony, a lesser necessarily included offense than 245(a), Penal le of California, as charged in COUNT I of the information.

FILED
OCT 25 1978
JOHN J. CORCORAN, Acting County Clerk
BY C. KAJIKAWA, DEPUTY

day of 19__,

---

66 FORM CR 290

ERIOR COURT OF CALIFORNIA, COUNTY OF LOS ANGELES
BRANCH NORTHEAST DIV.
ID. 9|0|0|0|5

FOR COURT USE ONLY

LE OF THE STATE OF CALIFORNIA versus
NDANT: 01 DAVIS GREGORY COPELAND [X] Present [ ] Not Present
AKA:
MITMENT TO STATE PRISON P.C. § 1170
RACT OF JUDGMENT CASE NUMBER: A 586961

ng 11-22-78 Dept. No. NEA Judge ROBERT M OLSON Clerk C KAJIKAWA
ter E AMAYA Counsel for People A STOVITZ
sel for Defendant D. FRAILEY Probation Number or Probation Officer UNK

fendant was convicted of the commission of the following crimes:
Additional counts are listed on attachment 1.a.

Code	Section No.	Crime	Date of Conviction Mo. Day Yr.	Jury Trial	Court Trial	Plea	Count Stayed PC § 654	PC § 12022 (a)or(b)	PC § 12022.5	PC § 12022.6(a)or(b)	PC § 12022.7	PC § 12022	PC § 12022.5	PC § 12022.6	PC § 12022.7
PC	12021	ASSAULT BY MEANS OF FORCE	10-25-78	x											

(ENHANCEMENTS Charged and Found: PC § 12022(a)or(b), PC § 12022.5, PC § 12022.6(a)or(b), PC § 12022.7; Additional term stricken due to circumstances in mitigation: PC § 12022, PC § 12022.5, PC § 12022.6, PC § 12022.7)

Number of prior prison terms charged and found: 0 667.5(c) felonies; 0 other than 667.5(c) felonies.
Punishment for prior prison terms stricken: ____ 667.5(c) felonies; ____ other than 667.5(c) felonies.
crime with the greatest "principal" term of imprisonment (including § 12022-series enhancements) is:
[ ] In the present proceeding, Count 02 B. [ ] In a prior uncompleted sentence identified on next line.
COUNTY CASE NUMBER COUNT CODE SECTION NUMBER CRIME AND DEGREE DATE OF CONVICTION MO. DAY YEAR
endant is sentenced on the crime with the greatest "principal" term to state prison for the [ ] lower [X] middle [ ] upper base term of 2 / Years
tayed and unstricken enhancements imposed:
[ ] Penal Code § 12022(a) [ ] Penal Code § 12022(b) [ ] Penal Code § 12022.5 [ ] Penal Code § 12022.7 .... Years.
[ ] Penal Code § 12022.6(a) [ ] Penal Code § 12022.6(b) .... Years.
[ ] Penal Code § 667.5(a) .... Years.
[ ] Penal Code § 667.5(b) .... Years.
erms for consecutive sentences:
1) [ ] Other convictions in the present case for felonies not listed in § 667.5(c) on counts .... 0 / years.
2) [ ] Other convictions in prior uncompleted sentences for felonies not listed in § 667.5(c)
COUNTY CASE NUMBER COUNTS .... 0 / years.
3) [ ] Other convictions in the present case for felonies listed in § 667.5(c) on counts .... 0 / years.
4) [ ] Other convictions in prior uncompleted sentences for felonies listed in § 667.5(c)
COUNTY CASE NUMBER COUNTS .... 0 / years.
urrent Sentences (to be served with sentence on count identified on line 3):
[ ] For convictions of the present case, counts ____ B. [ ] For convictions of prior uncompleted sentence.
ars imposed above on lines 4 through 5.E.(4), number of years stayed pursuant to California Rules of Court, Rule 447, to comply Penal Code §§ 1170.1(a) [5-year limit] and 1170.1(f) [double-base-term limit] .... (0 / years)
otal unstayed prison term imposed by this judgment is .... 2 / years.
ition of sentence imposed: A. [X] at initial sentencing hearing B. [ ] at resentencing pursuant to decision on appeal
C. [ ] after revocation of probation D. [ ] at resentencing pursuant to recall of commitment (P.C. § 1170(d))
ourt pronounced sentence on 1 1 2 2 7 8 (MO. DAY YEAR). Defendant is credited for time spent in custody, 231 total days, including:
Local Time 231 P.C. § 4019(b) credit ____, State Institutions Time ____ *(specify dates of admission and release in oral proceedings and minutes).*
dant is remanded to the custody of the Sheriff to be delivered: [X] forthwith [ ] after 48 hours, excluding Saturdays, Sundays and Holidays
he custody of the Director of Corrections at the Reception-Guidance Center located at [ ] Calif. Institution for Women – Frontera
[ ] Calif. Medical Facility – Vacaville [X] Calif. Institution for Men – Chino [ ] Other: (specify)

CORRECTED NUNC PRO TUNC AS PER MINUTE ORDER DATED JAN 19 1979

CLERK OF SUPERIOR COURT

I hereby certify the foregoing to be a correct abstract of the judgment made in this action.

By M. Aill... DEPUTY
Date 11-22-78

n is prescribed pursuant to Penal Code § 1213.5 to satisfy the requirements of Penal Code § 1213 (Abstract of ...

DATE AND TIME THIS REPORT	DATE PROPERTY BKD.	IF RELATED TO PREVIOUSLY BOOKED EVIDENCE, ORIG. EVID. BKD. TO (IN THIS CASE, COMPLETE ENTIRE REPORT)	DR
12-14-83 1400	12-14-83	Moore, Darrell A	83-12 0602

RESIDENCE ADDRESS: 8818 S Baring Cross Street
ARRESTEE: Davis, Gregory Copeland
DATE ORIGINAL EVIDENCE BKD.: 08-13-83
CHARGE BKD ON: 187PC-Mur
RESIDENCE ADDRESS (BUS. ADDRESS IF VICT. IS BUSINESS): 210 West 78th Street
BKG. # 7387 841
VICTIM: Moore, Darrell A
R- 971-4580
RESIDENCE ADDRESS: ------
OWNER OR IF UNKNOWN / FINDER: ----------
AREA OR CITY, & DATE CRIME OCCUR.: 77th 08-13-83
TYPE OF PREMISES: Residence
DEPT. EMPLOYEE IF BOOKED TO / SERIAL NO. / DIVISION
IF FIREARM, CRT CHECKS: AFS YES NO; NCIC YES NO
IS THIS STOLEN PROPERTY? Yes
PROBABLE CRIME: 187 PC
☒ FELONY ☐ MISD.
DATE & TIME PROP. TAKEN INTO POLICE CUSTODY — LOCATION — 12-14-83 0730 1220 E 74th Street
RD. OR CITY IF O: LA Count
INVESTIGATIVE UNIT: 77th Street Homicide
PROP. BKD. AT: 77th
NOTIFICATIONS - PERSONS & UNITS: SID/Slauson
CONNECTING REPORTS - TYPE & DR: Murder/Death/Arrest DR# same

Use Of Evidence Continuation: Use only with Arrest Report or, if no Arrest Report, with PIR. Do not use if evidence is related to previously booked evidence. To book evidence staple this page on top of Arrest face sheet (or PIR face sheet, if no arrest) and forward with evidence.

1. CIRCUMSTANCES (WHERE FOUND, BY WHOM, HOW MARKED, ETC.) EXPLAIN IF FOTO NOT ISSUED. GIVE RESULTS OF CRT CHECKS ON FIREARMS
2. ITEMIZE PROPERTY (LIST NARCOTICS FIRST, THEN MONEY, FIREARMS, PROPERTY WITH SERIAL NUMBERS, AND OTHER PROPERTY. IF RELATED TO PREVIOUSLY BKD. EVIDENCE, START WITH NEXT SEQUENTIAL ITEM NUMBER.)

The below listed items were recovered at 1220 East 74th Street pursuant to the follow up and service of an arrest warrant for Gregory Copeland Davis, charging 187 PC/Murder. Items #10 through #62, inclusive, were located by Detectives D. Richards #16633, L. Robert #10827, and L. Simms #12181 in the closet of the living room area.

Items #63 and #64 were seized by Detective Robert from a stand in the dining room area.

Item#65 was seized by Detective Simms from a rear bedroom. Detective J. Nunez #21435 was present when all items were removed and inventoried.

Evidence Booked:

ITEM NO.	QUAN.	ARTICLE	SERIAL NO./TYPE TEST OF DRUG	BRAND/DRUG WEIGHT, UNITS	MODEL NO./DRUG TEST RESULT	MISC.-COLOR, SIZE, INSCRIPTION, CALIBER, ETC. IF MULT. ARREST, INCL. NAME/BKG. * FROM WHOM TAKEN
10	1	Handgun	B 58562	Mondial	999	22 Caliber starter pistol 2" barrel
11	1	Handgun		Precise	880	22 Caliber starter pistol 2" barrel-blue steel
12	1	Handgun	0101695	Arminius	TitanTiger	38 Caliber revolver 2" barrel-blue steel

Preliminary Drug Test — SUPERVISOR/INVESTIGATING OFFICER TESTING — SERIAL NO. — WITNESSING OFFICER — SERIAL NO.
Search Warrant Info — DATE — ISSUED BY JUDGE — COURT NO. — ITEMS SEIZED PURSUANT TO WARRANT ☐ ALL ITEMS ☐ ONLY ITEM NOS.

SUPERVISOR APPROVING — SERIAL NO — PHOTO SSUED? ☐ YES ☐ NO
DATE & TIME REPRODUCED: 12-21-83 2225 — DIVISION: 12 — CLERK: 658

REPORTING EMPLOYEE(S)	SERIAL NO.	DIV	DETAIL
Det L Robert	10827	77th	Homi
Det J Nunez	21435	77th	Homi

PERSON REPORTING SIGNATURE: X

Property

83-12 06027

Quan.	Article	Serial No.	Brand	Model No.	Misc. Description (eg. color, size, inscriptions, caliber, revolver, etc)	Dollar Value
1	Handgun	026574	Clerke	22LR	22 Caliber revolver 2" barrel-chrome	
1	Handgun	2033572	RG		22 Caliber revolver 2" barrel-blue steel	
1	Handgun	W 81358	Colt	Agent	38 Caliber revolver 2" barrel-blue steel	
1	Handgun	14034	Smith/Wesson		32 Caliber revolver 4" barrel-chrome	
1	Handgun	455386	Browning	Automatic	25 Caliber automatic 2" barrel-blue steel	
1	Shotgun	387064	FIE		12 Gauge shotgun, sawed off 12½ inch barrel/17 inches overall	
1	Shotgun		JC Higgins	583.2	16 Gauge shotgun, bolt action sawed off, 15" barrel/26½" overall	
1	Shotgun		St Louis	1SS6 Sidetwist	12 Gauge shotgun, double barrel, 16" barrel	
1	Rifle		Winchester	67	22 Caliber long rifle sawed off, 12½" barrel/19" overall	
1	Rifle	SA 1256	Armi Jager Italy	APO 80	22 Caliber long rifle	
	Shotgun shells contained in a box		Federal (10) Remington (14)		12 Gauge #4 Red Plastic 12 Gauge #5 Green Plastic	
	Shotgun shells		Selby		12 Gauge #6 Black Plastic	
	Cartridges		W W		38 Caliber, lead (live) in a box	
	Cartridges		W W		22 Caliber, long rifle, copper jacket, boxed (live)	
	Cartridges		W W		22 Caliber, long rifle, copper jacketed (live)	
	Cartridges		Remington		32 Caliber, lead, boxed (live)	
	Cartridges		W W		25 Caliber, copper jacketed automatic, boxed (live)	

Continue on reverse side.

CONTINUATION SHEET

Property

83-12 06027

Item No.	Quan.	Article	Serial No.	Brand	Model No.	Misc. Description (eg. color, size, inscriptions, caliber, revolver, etc)	Dollar Value
30	4	Cartridges		Winchester		308 Caliber long rifle, silver tipped (live)	
31	1	Cartridge		Remington		38 Caliber, copper jacket hollow point, with dented primer (live)	
32	1	Cartridge		W W		38 Caliber, copper jacket (live)	
33	1	Cartridge		Remington		38 Caliber, brass with lead slug (live)	
34	2	Cartridges		W W		22 Caliber, short, copper jacketed (live)	
35	2	Cartridges		USC Co		32 Caliber WCF (live)	
36	1	Cartridge		Peters		25/20 Caliber (live)	

Items #31 through #36, inclusive, were placed into (1) envelope

Item No.	Quan.	Article	Serial No.	Brand	Model No.	Misc. Description	Dollar Value
37	6	Cartridges		R P		32 Caliber (4) short, lead (live) (2) long, lead	

Item #37 was removed from item #16.

Item No.	Quan.	Article	Serial No.	Brand	Model No.	Misc. Description	Dollar Value
38	7	Cartridges		W W		25 Caliber, copper jacketed automatic ammunition (live)	
39	1	Magazine				Black metal, browning auto	

Items #38 and #39 were removed from item #17.

Item No.	Quan.	Article	Serial No.	Brand	Model No.	Misc. Description	Dollar Value
40	1	Magazine				Black metal, 22 caliber, banana type	
41	1	Magazine				Black metal, 22 caliber, banana type	
42	19	Cartridges		W W		22 Caliber, long rifle copper jacketed	

Items #41 and #42 were loaded into item #22.

Item No.	Quan.	Article	Serial No.	Brand	Model No.	Misc. Description	Dollar Value
43	1	Bill of Sale				Made out to Gregory Davis for Cadillac Lic# 1 AHG 740	
44	1	Pawn Ticket 33353				From Shelly Jewelry & Loan 3800 S Western Ave 731 6483 for (1) ring, with large pea[rl]	

Continue on reverse side.

CONTINUATION SHEET

83-12 0[6027]

Item No.	Quan.	Article	Serial No.	Brand	Model No.	Misc. Description (eg. color, size, inscriptions, caliber, revolver, etc)	Dollar Value
45	1	Radio	961048	Concord	HPL 120	Car stereo, AM/FM, cas[sette] black plastic face	
46	1	Radio	8340254	King sonic		Car stereo, AM/FM, cassa[tte] black plastic face	
47	1	Beeper	416AGC6958	Motorola		Pocket pager, grey meta[l] case-assigned to Davis phone #292=2146	
	1	Tape recorder	2426447	Magnavox	1K0855	Reel to reel stereo, grey colored face 4-track	
	1	Equalizer		Rondo		Graphic equalizer, ampli[fier] black metal face	
	1	Trunk				Dark blue metal foot lock[er]	
	1	Attache case				grey plastic containing miscellaneous papers	
	1	Tape player		Roberts		8-track, stereo, tape player white metal face with brow[n] wooden case	
		Cardboard box				containing video machine accessories-VJT 250	
		Telephone		Muraphone	MP 301	Cordless extension telephon[e] tan colored plastic	
		Scale		Ohaus		Triple beam balance, tan in color with white metal.	
		Running Suit		J G Dee		Blue and white pants and jacket-front-"O.G." "Mr Batman", back-"Crip$", hood has "Cuz"	
		[B]andana				Dark blue in color with whi[te] print design (36X36)	
		[Ra]dio Scanner	000.813	Realistic	Pro 54	Patrolman scanning receiver black plastic case.	

Continue on reverse side.

CONTINUATION SHEET

83-12 060[27]

Item No.	Quan.	Article	Serial No.	Brand	Model No.	Misc. Description (eg. color, size, inscriptions, caliber, revolver, etc)	Dollar Value
59	1	Radio	03111497	Sanyo	C 2	AM/FM stereo, cassette player, brown and black plastic case.	
60	1	Turntable	235688	Symphonic	1013	Small black plastic tabl[e] with brown wooden case	
61	1	Television	643804-3	Magnavox		Star system, 19 inch color wooden case.	
62	1	Video cassette	317620521	RCA	VJT 250	Selectavision, green and black case (vhs)	
63	1	Audio mixer	217081199	Sansui	AX-7	Grey and black metal case	
64	1	Radio/Record Player	1015736	Sanyo	IXT 50	AM/FM stereo receiver cassette and turn table	
65	1	Radio	010381	Sanyo	M-X824	AM/FM Stereo cassette player, grey plastic case.	
66	3	Photo Albums				Containing various photographs and gang graffitti	

Item #66 was located in the living room closet by Detective Richards.

All the above items were inventoried and tagged. They were subsequently booked at 77th Street property.

Continue on reverse side.

CONTINUATION SHEET

Afterword

While his life sounds exciting, Batman is careful not to glorify it. Through telling his story, he hopes to prevent others from following the same path. He realizes that it is a miracle he made it out alive and is here to tell his story today.

On November 16, 2005, the L.A. County district attorney responded to Stanley "Tookie" Williams' petition for clemency. The report stated that "in 2004, the city of Los Angeles alone, gang crimes accounted for 291 homicides, 717 attempted homicides, 2,616 felony assaults, 61 attacks on police officers, 2,308 robberies, 44 kidnappings, 36 rapes, 754 acts of witness intimidation, 20 acts of extortion and 188 carjackings," and listed Tookie's early involvement with the Crips as one of the reasons why his clemency should be denied. "Although Stanley Williams is not directly responsible for every gang crime committed today, he was an integral founding member of a gang that has contributed, and continues to contribute, to the gang problem with devastating force." Governor Schwarzenegger denied clemency for Tookie, and stated that "there is also little mention or atonement in his writings… of the countless murders committed by the Crips following the lifestyle Williams once espoused. The senseless killing that has ruined many families, particularly African-American communities, in the name of the Crips and gang warfare is a tragedy of our modern culture."

Batman states, "Like they did with Tookie, people will blame me for the gang problem," Batman states. "They will say that I'm the reason why things are as bad as they are today. I understand what they're saying: I did play my part in the violence, but they've got to remember that the Baby Cribs was something we started to protect our neighborhood. The police weren't doing it, so we had to take matters into our own hands. Plus, when Raymond founded the Baby Cribs, we were all just kids: He was the oldest, at 15 years old, and I was just thirteen. We voted on who would be the leader by writing names on pieces of paper, and dropping them into a hat. Most of us were in Special Training and couldn't spell, so we just wrote the first letter of the person's name we wanted to vote for. Everyone voted for Raymond, and he became the leader. There was no master plan; we didn't intend for things to go the way they did, and even if we had been told how things would be some 40 years later, we probably wouldn't have believed it. We were just kids, doing what we thought was best at the time. So I don't regret being a founding member of the Crips. Things got violent later on, and I do regret parts of that, but not everything.

Greg 'Batman' Davis. 2009.

"However, I don't want kids to follow the same path that I did. Growing up on the Eastside in the 1960s and 1970s, there weren't a whole lot of options for me. Plus, I was slow and never got the help from teachers that I needed. I could have listened to my mom and dad tell me time and time again to leave the streets alone, but I didn't. I didn't think there was anything else for me to do, so I carried on. Things are different now; kids have a lot more opportunities. Obama proved that. Kids today have seen that they can be the president of the United States or anything they want to be. Of course, everybody can't be a basketball player, rapper or movie star, but there's plenty of other stuff kids can grow up to be too—doctors, lawyers, construction workers, barbers, store owners and so on.

Batman in prison. 1983.

"No job is promised them, but if they get an education, at least they will know how to fill out an application. But once they join a gang, they just mess their whole life up. Even if they escape prison or getting killed in the streets, they probably didn't get a proper education because they were too busy gangbanging, and might not even be able to fill out a job application.

Some gang members might be able to read and write, but what happens when they get to the part of the application that asks for previous work experience? They can't write gangbanging on there; they can't write down selling drugs. So they won't have nothing to write, and their application will get thrown straight in the trash.

"And when they get to a certain age, they'll be waiting on the mailman, looking for a retirement check. But there's no retirement check for gang members. In order to get a check in the mail, they had to put in their hours. If they didn't work, then there won't be any retirement checks coming in the mail when they get old. They need to work so that they will have some retirement money, otherwise they'll be walking around pushing baskets and looking for bottles. My mother used to say, 'Put something away for a rainy day.' That's still good advice. People want to floss and spend money on big jewels and pretty cars, but once that money is gone, that's it. Then they won't have a pot to piss in or a damn window to throw it of. I know about that from personal experience: I had lockers filled with cash, but I spent it on material things. Now that I'm older, I wish I had put that money into a house.

"That's why I say education is the most important thing. They got to have that or they won't ever have anything.

"That's why I say education is the most important thing. They got to have that or they won't ever have anything."

"And a lot of times, we like to blame it on the white man: 'We don't have anything because of him' and 'There's no hope'—well, that's an excuse. I used to think that way too, until I seen what I could accomplish. Everybody needs to stop saying 'we can't,' because we can.

"It was a long, hard journey for me. I was in and out of every correctional facility, and when I went to prison for the last time, I could have gotten multiple life sentences for the charges against me. But I made a deal with God, and I only had to do two years. God had a real big part in me getting where I am today.

Batman speaking at Reverend Price's church. 1994.

"I'm a true believer because there were so many times I could have been locked up for life or killed—I've been shot at, at point blank range, and not even had a scrape on me. It was a blessing that I could come out of it without getting hurt. But what happened to me does not happen for everyone. Other people might not get the same chances I had, so it's best to stay out of trouble in the first place. Like the saying goes, It's easy to get into trouble, but hard to get out of it. I know there were angels around me because there was something bigger for me to do.

"I can't save everybody, but if I can save one person at a time, then I know I'm doing a good job. That's the way I see it."

"God wanted me to help kids stay or get out of gangs, and that's what I've been doing. When I got out of prison for the last time, I started working at Fast Eddie's Steakhouse, which played the blues and drew an older crowd. Through hanging out there, I realized I needed to grow up. I met with a bishop, and started going to church. Then, in 1991, I met ex-football player Jim Brown, and started working for his Amer-I-Can Program. I went through a training process, and then Jim sent me to go work with kids in San Francisco for a year.

"I haven't looked back since.

"Throughout the 1990s, I continued to work for Amer-I-Can, and I also worked with non-profits like Project Corner Stone, Family Helpline and Jeopardy, the LAPD's gang intervention program, and I talked at schools and prisons around the country. I won a lot of awards for my work, including a Special Improvement Award, King Day Special Award of Achievement, a Certificate of Appreciation presented by James Hahn, and Bill Clinton even wrote me a letter to congratulate me on my achievements. Then, in 2000, I founded Let's Save the Babies, a non-profit that provides counseling to kids, promotes education and implements community programs, which I hope to continue in the future.

"I can't save everybody, but if I can save one person at a time, then I know I'm doing a good job. That's the way I see it."

This was the happiest day of my like marrying my lady Karen. I don't know where I would be without her.

IN THE COURT OF APPEAL OF THE STATE OF CALIFORNIA

SECOND APPELLATE DISTRICT, DIVISION FOUR

THE PEOPLE OF THE STATE OF CALIFORNIA,
Plaintiff and Respondent,
vs.
GREGORY COPELAND DAVIS,
Defendant and Appellant.

2D CRIM. 34505

APPELLANT'S OPENING BRIEF

STATEMENT OF THE CASE

In Information No. A586961 filed in Los Angeles Superior Court on May 2, 1978, Appellant was charged with assault by force and with deadly weapon, a violation of Penal Code Section 245a, and with violating Penal Code Section 12021 of the Dangerous Weapons' Control Law. (C.T. 1-2)

The Public Defender was appointed, and the Appellant pleaded not guilty. (C.T. 3)

Jury trial commenced on October 17, 1978, in Department NE A before the Honorable Robert M. Olson. (C.T. 21) On October 25, 1978, the jury returned with verdicts of not guilty as to the assault charge, and guilty as to the Dangerous Weapons' Control Law violation. (C.T. 61-63) On November 22, 1978, Appellant was sentenced to state prison and also filed a timely notice of appeal. (C.T. 65, 68)

LOS ANGELES, CALIFORNIA 90025
(213) 477-6519

POLICE

Westside Crip Antoinette.
Circa 1984.

Ced-Dog, Lowdown and Mr. Turtle in prison.
Circa 1984.

(Top) Big Crip Jackie and unknown woman, (Bottom) Lil Crip Jackie and unknown woman.
Circa 1986.

Unknowns.
Circa 1984.

The Homies.
Circa 1984.

6-9 Homies.
1983.

TQ and his girls chillin' on his Cadillac.
Circa 1982.

Lady TQ and friend with his Cadillac.
1982.

Batman in prison.
1984.

Jack, Batman and other guys in prison.
1984.

G-Man 69th Street in prison.
Circa 1984.

Harlem Crips.
Circa 1983.

DL Phil, Tyrone, Ghost and Batman at the skating rink.
1984.

Unknown, Cookie, Batman and Big Phil at the skating rink.
1985.

Lady TQ with AR15.
1984.

TQ with machine gun.
1984.

Homeboy Vegas Casino of Love by his lowrider.
1979.

Batman in front of a Cadillac on the eastside.
1981.

To Batman,
Kiss!!!

Rita
857-0726

To
Batman,
Watch out
for Robin.
It might be me
Kiss
Cheré

NBT795
24 Hour Photography
By Joe (213) 745-2551
"We'll shoot anything...anywhere"

Stephanie

To Greg:
From:
757-9930

Batman and friends.
1985.

Mama Kim, Batman and Mama Kim's daughter at the Steakhouse.
1985.

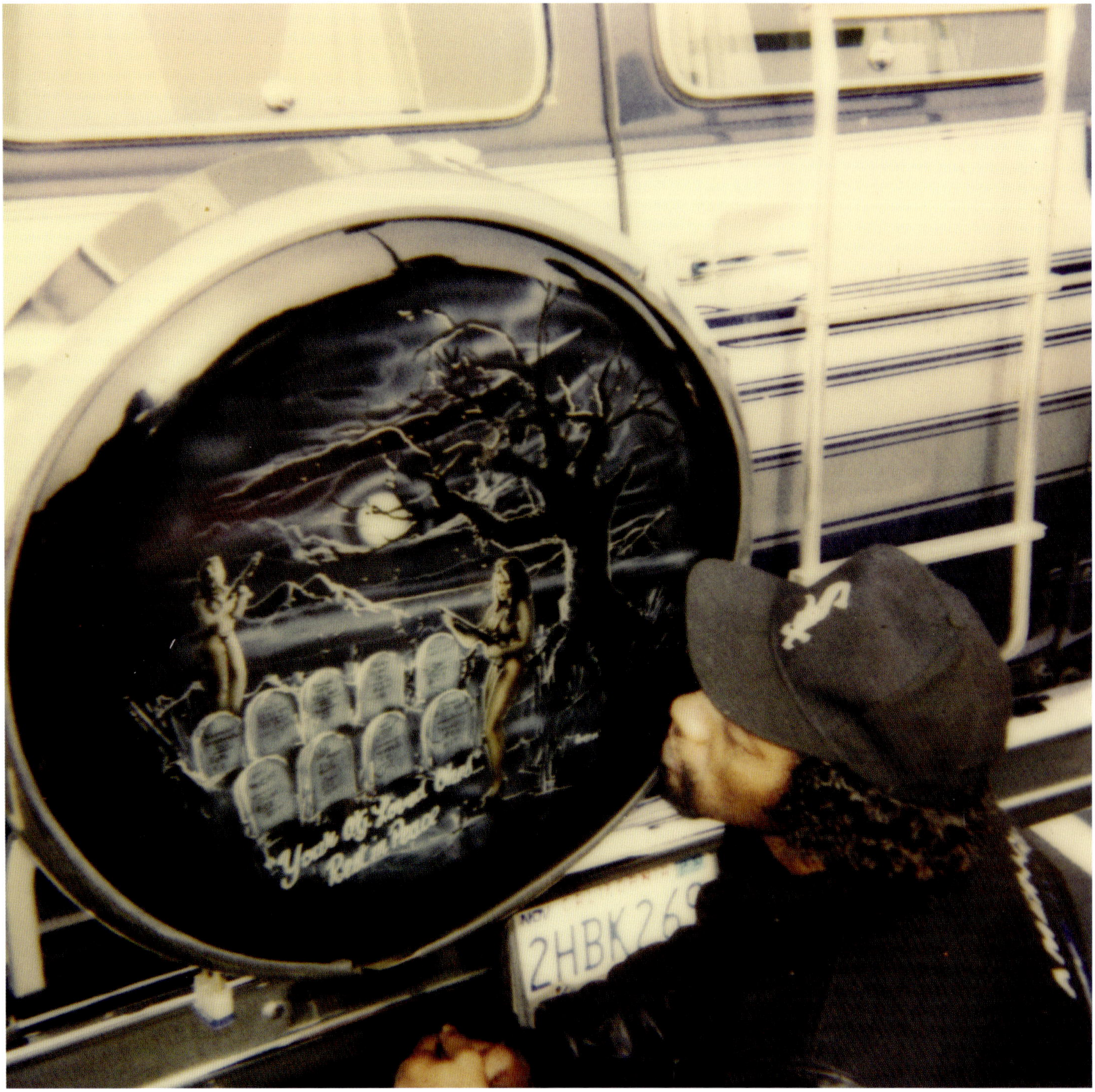

Batman and his 1987 Chevy van.
1987.

Batman and his van.
1992.

Big Poppa, Batman and Dollar Bill at the Steakhouse.
1984.

Batman with bulletproof vest and a .38 at the Steakhouse.
1984.

APRIL
ANYONE WISHES

NO PROFANITY
NO LOITERING
THANK YOU

ABSTRACT OF JUDGMENT – COMMITMENT
SINGLE OR CONCURRENT COUNT FORM
(Not to be used for Multiple Count Convictions nor Consecutive Sentences)

FORM DSL 2

SUPERIOR COURT OF CALIFORNIA, COUNTY OF LOS ANGELES

BRANCH CENTRAL CRIMINAL

COURT I.D. 1 9 0 0 0 1

PEOPLE OF THE STATE OF CALIFORNIA versus

DEFENDANT: DAVIS, GREGORY

AKA:

[X] PRESENT [ ] NOT PRESENT

COMMITMENT TO STATE PRISON ABSTRACT OF JUDGMENT [ ] AMENDED ABSTRACT

CASE NUMBER: A398462

DATE OF HEARING (MO) (DAY) (YR)	DEPT. NO.	JUDGE	CLERK
07 30 84	133	HENRY P NELSON	R ZAGON

REPORTER	COUNSEL FOR PEOPLE	COUNSEL FOR DEFENDANT	PROBATION NO. OR PROBATION OFFIC
C MATTINGLY	R MAYER	E BARON	X010966

1. DEFENDANT WAS CONVICTED OF THE COMMISSION OF THE FOLLOWING FELONY:

COUNT	CODE	SECTION NUMBER	CRIME	YEAR CRIME COMMITTED	DATE OF CONVICTION MO	DAY	YEAR	CONVICTION BY JURY TRIAL	COURT TRIAL	PLEA	TERM (L,M,U)	TIME IMPOSED YEARS	MONT
1	PC	12020(a)	POSS SAW-OFF SHOTGUN	83	05	23	84			X	M	2	

2. ENHANCEMENTS (CHARGED AND FOUND, STRICKEN, TIME IMPOSED):

COUNT	12022(a) C/F	S	I	12022(b) C/F	S	I	12022.3(a) C/F	S	I	12022.3(b) C/F	S	I	12022.5 C/F	S	I	12022.6(a) C/F	S	I	12022.6(b) C/F	S	I	12022.7 C/F	S	I	12022.8 C/F	S	I	C/F	S	I

3. OTHER ORDERS:

STAY OF EXECUTION GRANTED TO AUGUST 6, 1984.

4. A. NUMBER OF PRIOR PRISON TERMS:

§	C/F	S	I
667.5(a)	0	0	0
667.5(b)	0	0	0
667.6(b)	0	0	0

B. NUMBER OF PRIOR FELONY CONVICTIONS:

§	C/F	S	I
667.6(a)	0	0	0

5. TIME STAYED § 1170.1(f) [DOUBLE BASE LIMIT]:

6. TOTAL TERM IMPOSED: → 2

7. [ ] THIS SENTENCE IS TO RUN CONCURRENT WITH ANY PRIOR UNCOMPLETED SENTENCE(S).

8. EXECUTION OF SENTENCE IMPOSED:

A. [X] AT INITIAL SENTENCING HEARING B. [ ] AT RESENTENCING PURSUANT TO DECISION ON APPEAL C. [ ] AFTER REVOCATION OF PROBATION D. [ ] AT RESENTENCING PURSUANT TO RECALL OF COMMITMENT [PC §1170(d)]

9. DATE SENTENCE PRONOUNCED: MO 07 DAY 30 YEAR 84

CREDIT FOR TIME SPENT IN CUSTODY: TOTAL DAYS 259 INCLUDING: ACTUAL LOCAL TIME 173 LOCAL CONDUCT CREDITS 86 STATE INSTITUTIONS [ ] DMH [ ] CDC

10. DEFENDANT IS REMANDED TO THE CUSTODY OF THE SHERIFF, TO BE DELIVERED:

[ ] FORTHWITH

[X] AFTER 48 HOURS, EXCLUDING SATURDAYS, SUNDAYS AND HOLIDAYS

INTO THE CUSTODY OF THE DIRECTOR OF CORRECTIONS AT THE RECEPTION-GUIDANCE CENTER LOCATED AT:

[ ] CALIF. INSTITUTION FOR WOMEN — FRONTERA [ ] CALIF. MEDICAL FACILITY — VACAVILLE [X] CALIF. INSTITUTIO FOR MEN — CHINO

[ ] OTHER (SPECIFY):

CLERK OF SUPERIOR COURT

hereby certify the foregoing to be a correct abstract of the judgment made in this action.

DEPUTY'S SIGNATURE [signature] DATE AUG 3 - 1984

his form is prescribed pursuant to Penal Code §1213.5 to satisfy the requirements of Penal Code §1213 (Abstract of Judgment and Commitment) for determinat entences under Penal Code §1170. A copy of probation report shall accompany the Department of Corrections' copy of this form pursuant to Penal Code §1203 copy of the sentencing proceedings and any supplementary probation report shall be transmitted to the Department of Corrections pursuant to Penal Cod 1203.01. Attachments may be used but must be incorporated by reference.

Form Adopted by the udicial Council of California ffective July 1, 1981

ABSTRACT OF JUDGMENT – COMMITMENT
SINGLE OR CONCURRENT COUNT FORM
(Not to be used for Multiple Count Convictions nor Consecutive Sentences)

FORM DSL 290.1

Pen. C. 1213.5

SUPERIOR COURT OF THE STATE OF CALIFORNIA
FOR THE COUNTY OF LOS ANGELES

The People of the State of California, Plaintiff, v. GREGORY COPELAND DAVIS, Defendant.	No. A398462 INFORMATION VIO. DANGEROUS WEAPONS' CONTROL LAW (Sec. 12020(a), P.C.) - CTS. I - IV VIO. SEC. 12021, P.C.- CTS. V - VIII

The said GREGORY COPELAND DAVIS

is accused by the District Attorney of and for the County of Los Angeles, State of California, by this information, of the crime of **VIOLATION OF DANGEROUS WEAPONS' CONTROL LAW**, Section 12020(a), Penal Code of California, a felony, committed as follows:

That the said GREGORY COPELAND DAVIS

on or about the 14th day of December, 1983,

at and in the County of Los Angeles, State of California, did willfully and unlawfully manufacture, cause to be manufactured, import into the State of California, keep for sale, offer and expose for sale, and give, lend, and possess an instrument and weapon of the kind commonly known as a sawed-off shotgun (FIE Brand shotgun, serial No. 387064: less than 26" in length and barrel less than 8").

SIX ...

JOHN K. VAN DE KAMP, District Attorney
for the County of Los Angeles, State of California

By .... Deputy

8-21-84

Filed in open Superior Court of the State of California, County of Los Angeles, on motion of the District Attorney of said County.

DATED:

JOHN J. CORCORAN, Clerk

By ____________ Deputy

761546M1—Rev. 9/80—10/80

DISTRICT OFFICE
100 PASEO DE SAN ANTONIO
SAN JOSE CALIFORNIA 95113
(408) 288-7515

CAPITOL OFFICE
STATE CAPITOL
P O BOX 942849
SACRAMENTO, CA 94249-0001
TEL AREA CODE 916
445-4253

Assembly
California Legislature

JOHN VASCONCELLOS
ASSEMBLYMAN, TWENTY-SECOND DISTRICT
CHAIRMAN
COMMITTEE ON WAYS AND MEANS

HIGHER EDUCATION
AGRICULTURE
BANKING AND FINANCE

ASSEMBLY DEMOCRATIC
ECONOMIC PROSPERITY TEAM

April 19, 1994

Gregory Davis
Amer-I-Can
222 Schwerin, Apt. 210
San Francisco, CA 94134

Greg -

Thank you very much for your participation at the annual self-esteem day. Your presentation was enlightening and clearly enhanced the educational benefits of the event.

If we are to reduce crime and rehabilitate individuals, self-esteem must be recognized as the key to crime prevention. All of the featured programs incorporate self-esteem as a major component and their success lies in the fact that they empower the participants to help themselves, thereby encouraging them to act responsibly toward others.

I hope that your dedication and commitment have been further charged by this event, and I encourage you to continue your meaningful work with great zeal.

I wish you well.

THE WHITE HOUSE

WASHINGTON

December 11, 2000

It gives me great pleasure to congratulate Chiquita Tolton and Gregory Davis as you are honored by "Let's Save the Babies" as Woman and Man of the Year.

You have worked with energy and dedication to provide solutions to the many problems that young people face in today's society. With your active involvement, you have brought hope and help to many families in need. I commend each of you for your commitment to the American ideal of service. Your work is going a long way toward healing and renewing the communities you serve, inspiring all who seek to improve our society.

Best wishes for every future success.

Bill Clinton

Compiled & edited by: Roger Gastman
Written by: Zio Fulcher
Art Direction: Shane Jessup
Scanning & production: Deanna Guzman, Leon Catfish & Francesca Quintano
Batman logo by: Jason Filipow
Special thanks: Nemo & Sara Rosen

www.gregbatmandavis.com

Library of Congress Control Number: 2012934432

ISBN: 978-0-7643-4206-6
Printed in China

Schiffer Books are available at special discounts for bulk purchases for sales promotions or premiums. Special editions, including personalized covers, corporate imprints, and excerpts can be created in large quantities for special needs. For more information contact the publisher:

Published by Schiffer Publishing Ltd.
4880 Lower Valley Road
Atglen, PA 19310
Phone: (610) 593-1777; Fax: (610) 593-2002
E-mail: Info@schifferbooks.com

For the largest selection of fine reference books on this and related subjects, please visit our website at **www.schifferbooks.com**
We are always looking for people to write books on new and related subjects. If you have an idea for a book, please contact us at
proposals@schifferbooks.com

This book may be purchased from the publisher.
Please try your bookstore first.
You may write for a free catalog.

In Europe, Schiffer books are distributed by
Bushwood Books
6 Marksbury Ave.
Kew Gardens
Surrey TW9 4JF England
Phone: 44 (0) 20 8392 8585; Fax: 44 (0) 20 8392 9876
E-mail: info@bushwoodbooks.co.uk
Website: www.bushwoodbooks.co.uk

Batman at the Snooty Fox.
1984.

MR
OG
BATMAN
DA
EAST SIDE
GANG
IN

$ BATMAN $
Raiders
$ TUZ $

DEDICATIONS

I want to thank God for letting me be here and giving me strength. Without God in your heart, who would you have; who could you trust? We all have to go through trials and tribulations, but I made it through the storm and the rain. Thank you, Father.

I dedicate this to Sarah, my grandmother, who believed in me when things went wrong. When other family members put me down, she was always there for me. She did the best she could for her grandkids. Church-going folks. If we were sick, we didn't have to go to school, but when Sunday came she'd say, "We goin' to Church, God will heal you." I miss my grandmother.

To Mr. and Mrs. Davis. Momma and daddy. I know you tried to keep me out of trouble. But a hard head will make a soft behind.

Daddy, some peoples will say all the punishments and whoopins you gave me is child abuse, but like the Bible says, "Spare the rod." You did a good job of keeping me here. And I love you for it, and I respect you for it.

Momma, me and you are going to have some good times together traveling. When I asked you to go with me to speak to the kids at churches and schools, or whatever it was, you never told me no. You and daddy never turned your back on me. I appreciate it. I love you.

To a special lady, my wife. I remember the first time I met you and I had just came home from prison. I thought I was all that, big chest, big arms, blue rag tied around the face, with my locs on my head, driving a 500 SEL. I followed you to a gas station, was hollerin' at you, you looked at me like I was crazy. You said to me, "What are you doing? Is you a gang member?" and I answered, "Yeah." I asked you for you number, you gave it to me and I left. I called you and you told me what people were saying about me. They said to you don't get involved with him, but you followed your heart. Look what God has done for me and you. No one can take your place. You are a very sweet, loving wife. Quiet, respectable and I love it! I love you, Karen Davis.

To a very, very close friend. When I was down you were there for me. When I asked you never said no. That's what I call a friend. You treat me like family. You never turned your back on me. I would never forget you. Some people never know what blessings are. I appreciate it. We broke bread together. We went to art shows together and you were in my corner all the way. And it don't stop, we're going to keep pushing until you become an actor and producer. So you know I'm here for you on whatever. Love you, Kevin Chhann.

Batman's mother and father.
Date unknown.

Batman and Karen.
1988.

To my loved ones on Death Row, I ain't forgot about you:

Cain
PotatoHead
Money
Romeo
NoNo
Slan
Hassan
Nutty
Lil Ken Dog
Rabbit
Baby Rerm
Dirty
C.W.
Lil Fee
Treach
Evil
Herc
Grandpa
And the ones names I can't think of that's on the Row, much love and I'm praying for all you guys that one day you'll come home.

All the homies that's walking the line:

Black Johnnie
Sweet Pea
Big Cesar
Big Bob
Tweety Bird
Big Boo
Lightbulb
Big Ant
Stacey
Big Bam
Ronnie Bam
Cutes
Turtle
Verdus Swan
Big Bean
Key
Big Buster
Eddie Haythorne
Ken Dog
Bobby Lucas
Sad
Speedy
Snoop
Bimbo
Frank Freemon
T-Manual
Ace Capone
Big Bub
LaLa
Bitter Dog Bruno
Lumberjack
Bad Habit Rabbit
Lil Sad
Dog
Big Ace
Tony
Sam
Big Looney
Bitter Child
Mad Forehead
Big Devil
Mumbles
Old Man
Dirt Down
Dynomite
Wayne with no Brains
Kenny Carter
Doc Roc
BeBe
Gucci
Puppet
Chile
Big Rick
Dirty Red

All my loved ones rest in peace:

Raymond
Craig
Crazy Crip
Donni BoBo
Herc
Mad Bull
Pet Bull
Lil Pet Bull
Lil Batman
Mad Dog
Mack Thomas
Took
Bobby
Big C
Hot Rod
Big Papa
Duck
James Miller
Oldie
Big Mouse
Rusty
Quake
Turtle
Onion
Ricky Silent
Termite
Salty
Budda
Doc Thone
Dave
T-Tiger
Gangsta John
Iron Man
Ju Rock
Lil Smokey
Weasel
Big Phil
Cadillac Jim
Big Bunchie
Dee Dee
Terry Simmons
Chipper
Chocolate
Run Away
Michael Johnson
Godfather
Jelly Bean
Lil Crazy Crip
Slow
Heron
Eckie
Chile
Gypsy
Tweety
UT- Undertaker
Criptone
Cripcal
Big Bob
Mack
Big Pysch
Asmo
Bub
Mo
Terry Brown
Cody Brown
Larry
And for those I can't think of, rest in peace.

Special acknowledgements:

Rosie Grier
Ice-T
Jim Brown
Magic Johnson
LJ Reynolds
Maxine Waters
Stephanie Wanzo
Lynda Stewart
Deborah Davis
Killah Priest
Snoop Dogg
Philip McCain
Lapica
Earthquake
TQ
Tyson
Nemo
Willie Flag
Rockhead
Fast Black
Frog
Big Bub
Big Twin
Anita Chhann
Queen Latifah
Owl
Deadeye
Bubbalicious
Buck
Black Dog
Big Alder
Chrome
Big G
Gator
Tony Mohamed
Spike
Lil James
Sweet Back
Fast Eddie
Andre Davis
James J
Pyscho Michael
Rat
Kenny McKnight
Donnie Washington
Melvin Hardy
Angela Davis
David Heeley
Apache
Barefoot Pookie
Blue
Boon
Bopete
Chico
Clint
Cool Breeze
Fat Rat
Geronimo Pratt
Bunchy Carter
Ghetto
Warlock
Half Pint
Little Ace
Monkeyman
Marty
Mustafa
Nelson Mandela
Side Winder
Skull
Tony Stacey
Walt
Bird
Camasse
Lee Arthur
Hewie
Baby Jay
Mary J. Blige
Ever Brinker
Slim
P.P.
Big Ship
Louis Farrakhan
Malcolm X
Van
Willis Shobe
George
PeeWee
Caveman
Brenda Sycks
Barbara
King Swift
Ray Willis
Big Zoom
Kawana
Van
Ms. Esther
Fred Williams
Ron Overtree

Shout out to the OG Criplettes:

Jackie Tide
Pam Tide
Lil Pam
Dee Dee
Crip Jackie
Black Connie
Bonnie
Catwoman
Lady Breeze
Stacie
Kelly
Lady Bull
Green Eye
Claudette
Hot Tail
Big Lynn
Terry Dent
Cheetah
Latanya
Michelle

My spiritual advisor

Bishop T.D. Jake,
Keep up the good work.

Steak House

Batman and Mike at Youth Authority during a visit from the girls. 1974.

Greg 'Batman' Davis. Photo by Adam Wallacavage. 2009.

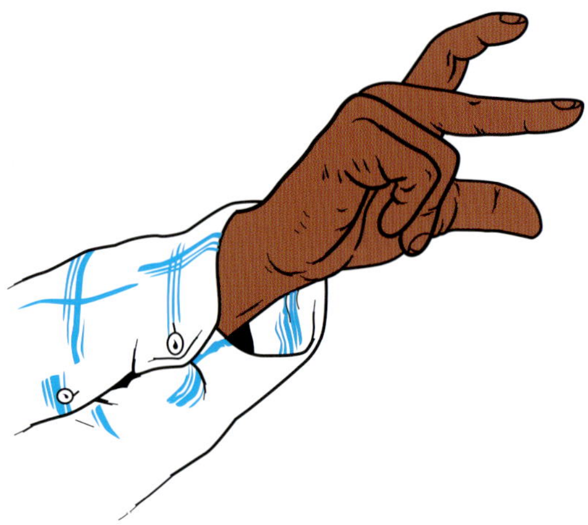